Nos encantan las ciencias
So Into Science!

EXPLOREMOS EL ACUARIO

EXPLORING THE AQUARIUM

Marie Roesser
Traducido por / Translated by Eida de la Vega

Gareth Stevens
PUBLISHING

Please visit our website, www.garethstevens.com. For a free color catalog of all our high-quality books, call toll free 1-800-542-2595 or fax 1-877-542-2596.

Library of Congress Cataloging-in-Publication Data

Names: Roesser, Marie, author.
Title: Exploring the aquarium = Exploremos el acuario / Marie Roesser.
Description: New York : Gareth Stevens Publishing, [2019] | Series: So into science! = Nos encantan las ciencias | Includes index.
Identifiers: LCCN 2018013145| ISBN 9781538236321 (library bound)
Subjects: LCSH: Aquariums–Juvenile literature. | Aquarium animals–Juvenile literature.
Classification: LCC SF457.3 .R64 2019 | DDC 639.34–dc23
LC record available at https://lccn.loc.gov/2018013145

Published in 2019 by
Gareth Stevens Publishing
111 East 14th Street, Suite 349
New York, NY 10003

Translator: Eida de la Vega
Editor, English: Therese Shea
Designer: Sarah Liddell

Photo credits: Cover, p. 1 (aquarium) ZullU InFocus/Shutterstock.com; cover, pp. 1 (fish), 7 Grigorev Mikhail/Shutterstock.com; p. 5 Evgeniia Ozerkina/Shutterstock.com; p. 9 Anna Moskvina/Shutterstock.com; pp. 11, 24 (alligator) Nagel Photography/Shutterstock.com; p. 13 Vlad61/Shutterstock.com; pp. 15, 24 (seahorse) Vladimir Wrangel/Shutterstock.com; p. 17 kelldallfall/Shutterstock.com; p. 19 f11photo/Shutterstock.com; p. 21 blue-sea.cz/Shutterstock.com; p. 23 Pavel L Photo and Video/Shutterstock.com.

Printed in the United States of America

CPSIA compliance information: Batch #CW19GS: For further information contact Gareth Stevens, New York, New York at 1-800-542-2595.

Contenido

Contents

¡Este es el acuario!
Vemos animales
que viven en el agua.

This is the aquarium!
We see animals
that live in water.

Algunos animales
viven en agua dulce.
¡Veo peces
de agua dulce!

....

Some animals live
in freshwater.
I see freshwater fish!

Vemos nutrias de río.
Ellas juegan en los ríos.

....

We see river otters.
They play in rivers!

Vemos un aligátor.
Se esconde.
¡Sus ojos y hocico
sobresalen!

....

We see an alligator.
It hides.
Its eyes and nose
stick out!

Algunos animales
viven en agua salada.
¡Veo peces
de agua salada!

Some animals live
in salty water.
I see saltwater fish!

Vemos caballitos de mar.
¡Son peces!

We see seahorses.
They are fish!

Vemos un pez vela.
¡Es el pez más rápido!

We see a sailfish.
It's the fastest fish!

Vemos un tiburón ballena.
¡Es el pez más grande!

....

We see a whale shark.
It's the largest fish!

Vemos una tortuga marina.
Las tortugas marinas ponen huevos en la playa.

....

We see a sea turtle.
Sea turtles lay eggs on the beach.

¡He aprendido mucho!

I learned so much!

Palabras que debes aprender
Words to Know

(el) aligátor
alligator

(el) caballito de mar
seahorse

Índice / Index